Prayers
for
Sleepless
Nights

Helen Reichert Lambin

PUBLICATIONS

PRAYERS FOR SLEEPLESS NIGHTS
Helen Reichert Lambin

Edited by Andrew Yankech
Cover design by Tom A. Wright
Text Design and typesetting by Patricia A. Lynch

Scripture quotations are from the *New Revised Standard Version Bible*, copyright © 1989 by the Division of Christian Education of the National Council of the Churches of Christ in the USA. Used by permission. All rights reserved.

Copyright © 2009 by Helen Reichert Lambin

Published by ACTA Publications, 5559 W. Howard Street, Skokie, IL 60077-2621, (800) 397-2282, www.actapublications.com

Library of Congress Number: 2009930510
ISBN: 978-0-87946-405-9
Printed in The United States by Versa Press
Year 16 15 14 13 12 11 10 09
Printing 10 09 08 07 06 05 04 03 02 First Edition

Topics

Anxieties 10

Bills, Bread and Boundaries 12

Busy Business 14

Change and Changes 16

Children 18

Confusion.. 20

Decisions 22

Discouragement and the Dark Hours 24

Faith and Doubts 26

Forgiveness 28

Friends in High Places.. 30

Friends in Low Places 32

Gifts and Grace 34

Gratitude and Joyful Noise 36

Growing Old-er Without Growing Old 38

Hearth, Heart and Home....................................... 40

Holidays and Hallowed Days.................................. 42

Illness... 44

Journeys 46

Just As I Am.. 48

Learning Curves 50

Letting Go 52

Loss and Sorrow 54

Nightly News 56

Perspective 58

Prayer and Presence 60

Regrets 62

Relationships 64

Resentment and Anger 66

Sleep and Relaxation 68

Unappreciated, Depreciated Me 70

Working 72

Working Things Out, or Plan B 74

Welcome Morning 76

For my parents, Verto and Helen G. Reichert,
who introduced me to the meaning of prayer and faith—
in the big events, good and bad,
in the undecided, and in everyday life.

To Gregory Augustine Pierce, man of books,
who writes about and fosters this meaning.

And to all my fellow insomniacs:
Peace be with you, tonight.

Introduction

If you've been there you already know it. Sleepless nights are hard. They can be harder still when they come after—or worse yet, before—difficult days. It is as though we conduct a solitary rehearsal for tomorrow's problems in the middle of the night. We are the director; we are the writers, constantly editing and revising the script in our heads; and we act it out in our minds. Of course, it almost never plays out the way we scripted it.

I know…like you, I've spent many sleepless nights wrestling with the small details of the day—and the larger questions of life. Yet, in spite of the fact that I certainly didn't choose this unwanted wakefulness, in some ways it has turned out to be a gift. Over time, and over many a long night, I started having conversations with God that have taken me to surprising places. *Prayers for Sleepless Nights* arose out of those conversations. We want to be, and are supposed to be, asleep. Everyone else in the world is. Well, as it turns out, many of them are not. It is for them—for you—that I have written this book.

So why not do something with this newfound, if unwelcome, time? There is a lot to be said for prayer in the night. Nighttime is usually quieter, there are fewer distractions, and you probably feel less guilt over not doing something "constructive"—as if prayer were not constructive in its own right. At the same time, life can look quite different at night. Things that seemed minor by day can loom much larger, and things that already loom large by day can cast a suffocating shadow at night. But there's light even in the darkness, because we are not there alone.

I sometimes think of God's presence during long, sleepless nights as something along the lines of those fund-raising telecasts, where the announcer says, "We have someone standing by waiting to take your call." Clearly, that's a theological over-simplification of God's presence, but it certainly points in the right direction. Someone is perfectly ready and willing to take our call. And "perfectly" is the operative word. The psalmists figured this out several thousand years ago. Whether song, poetry, praise or lament, the psalms reflect a sense of personal conversation with the Divine. Thousands of years ago, people were evidently feeling many of the same emotions we feel today, and they called upon faith to get through it and grow from it.

The prayers in this book are prayers of friendship, of companionship with God. They are not intended as sleep aids—although it would be nice if it worked out that way! Rather, they are intended as possibilities for you to make use of your wakeful times and wandering thoughts. After all, you are awake. God is awake. And God is there for you.

Each of the prayers is followed by a scripture quote for your reflection. My hope is that you will use these prayers and scripture reflections as a starting point for your own prayers. At the end of each topic is a section for "My Prayers," where you can jot down your own thoughts and prayers. You may want to keep a notebook nearby so you can write as much as you like. Remember that your prayers don't have to be elegant or formal. The God who loves and hears us is there to receive our thoughts, words and feelings. Just like the close friend or family member to whom you can pour out your thoughts and emotions, God is there to receive your stream of consciousness, no matter the time of day or night. Think of your words as part of your conversation with God, just as the psalmist who wrote the lines below did. Perhaps he or she had also experienced his or her fair share of sleepless nights before writing these words in prayer:

Let my prayer be counted as incense before you,
and the lifting up of my hands as an evening sacrifice.
(Psalm 141:2)

Prayers for Sleepless Nights

Anxieties

There are as many reasons for being awake and anxious in the middle of the night as there are people who are awake. And, as if other anxieties aren't enough, there is the plain fact that you are awake when everyone else is, theoretically, asleep. It may not be fair. It certainly isn't fun. But it doesn't have to be futile.

✵ Night Watches

Midnight, one o'clock, one thirty, two o'clock. Should I look at those little lighted numbers again? No. Yes. No. What, only fifteen minutes have passed? Will morning ever come? Faithful Friend who watches over me in the day hours, are you also there with me in this endless night?

> One is calling to me from Seir, "Sentinel, what of the night? Sentinel, what of the night?" The sentinel says: "Morning comes, and also the night. If you will inquire, inquire; come back again." (Isaiah 21:11-12)

✵ Jitters

If I were not so jittery, Lord, maybe I could pray. To be honest, if I were not so jittery, maybe I'd be asleep instead of thinking about praying. Lord Jesus, help me do one or the other. But if it's all the same to you, at this moment I'd go for sleep. I ask you, who can calm waves and disciples, how do I calm myself?

> I will both lie down and sleep in peace;
> for you alone, O Lord, make me lie down in safety.
> (Psalm 4:8)

Complaint Department

It does seem, dear God, that it is in the late watches of the night that things catch up with me. And it does seem that it is then that I turn to you. It's not that I want to burden you, patient God, when I'm disturbed with my world, or when I'm disturbed with me. But who better to turn to? Who can better deal with me being me?

> *With my voice I cry to the Lord; with my voice I make supplication to the Lord. I pour out my complaints before him; I tell my trouble before him. When my spirit is faint, you know my way. (Psalm 142:1-3)*

MY PRAYERS

Bills, Bread and Boundaries

Talking about money can be awkward, and praying about it even more so. The people who say that money isn't everything are usually those who have more than enough. Anyone struggling to pay the bills or to put food on the table feels the importance of money. The problems begin when money matters too much and the needs of others don't matter enough. The ancient authors of Scripture and theologians of the present both talk about divine compassion for the poor, who are always in God's heart of hearts. But both also point out that the needs of the poor are in human hands—yours and mine.

Bills

There are a lot of things I'd rather talk to you about, God, than money. But tonight, at this moment, it's hard to think of anything else. The bills are there; the money isn't. It's not that I am asking for luxuries. I'm talking about the bill for the rent or the mortgage, for health insurance, for groceries, for transportation, to get to work...to find work. And, I must admit, it would be nice to have a little left over, maybe, for some small luxuries for my family, for me, and for others in need. What can I say? I can only bring my prayer to you, Giver of Surprising Gifts.

Pray then in this way: Our Father in heaven...
Give us this day our daily bread. (Matthew 6:9, 11)

Their Daily Bread

God, as in so many things, I'm "in between." I am not poor, but neither am I rich. Some people would say that I'm part of the vanishing middle class. All I know is that I'm lucky to be there. I also know that the balance is tipping a lot of people to poor. So, Giver of Life, what is my role here? Help me find the wisdom to recognize the lines between need, wish and greed, and the generosity of spirit to act on it.

They asked only one thing, that we remember the poor,
which was actually what I was eager to do. (Galatians 2:10)

❀ Fail Scale

What a way to look at things: To measure people by how much money they make—or don't make. By that scale, God, so many good people would be judged failures. Or, worse yet, they might judge themselves that way. God of Justice, help me to rebalance my scales with your wisdom and vision. And bless all the "failures" with a fair new day.

Talk no more so very proudly, let not arrogance come from your mouth; for the Lord is a God of knowledge, and by him actions are weighed. (1 Samuel 2:3)

MY PRAYERS

Busy Business

Do you remember the frantic White Rabbit in *Alice in Wonderland*? He was always darting here, there and everywhere, looking at his watch and bemoaning that he was late (as the film version put it, "for a very important date"). What he was late for was unspecified, but he was always just passing through, fast. And frazzled. Maybe you can identify with the White Rabbit even, or especially, in the darkness of night.

❈ To-Do List

There are a million things to do tomorrow…or is it already today? Work, errands, family, pets, friends, self, responsibilities, volunteer projects, personal projects, unfinished tasks. And, in between, I was going to learn Spanish, Swahili, German; write a poem, a novel, an article; learn to play the recorder, the harmonica, the kazoo. I seem to have this Martha-type life, when I would like to have some Mary-like time to sit at your feet, Brother Jesus, and listen—if only I didn't have so much to do. But not right now, not at this moment. So I ask you, Friend of the Dark Hours, give me a Mary night before I begin my Martha day.

> *Now as they went on their way, he entered a certain village, where a woman named Martha welcomed him into her home. She had a sister named Mary, who sat at the Lord's feet and listened to what he was saying. But Martha was distracted by her many tasks; so she came to him and asked, "Lord, do you not care that my sister has left me to do all the work by myself? Tell her then to help me." But the Lord answered her, "Martha, Martha, you are worried and distracted by many things; there is need of only one thing. Mary has chosen the better part, which shall not be taken away from her." (Luke 10:38-41)*

❈ Tomorrow and Tomorrow and …

So much to do tomorrow, dear God. So much left undone today. Yesterday, today, tomorrow. Running, running, running, and no finish line in sight. Steadfast God, you live in eternity where time is unmeasured. Give me the gift of some quiet times. And help me to live in the moment, in this moment, even if this moment is tonight.

> *Come now, you who say, "Today or tomorrow we will go to such and such a town and spend a year there, doing business and making money." Yet you do not even know what tomorrow will bring. What is your life? You are a mist that appears for a little while and then vanishes. Instead you ought to say, "If the Lord wishes, we will live and do this or that." (James 4:13-15)*

❈ Working at Sleeping

It's late, patient God. Growing later by the minute. I can't get to sleep. And I have to get up and get going tomorrow. At five. Six. Seven. Even if I fell asleep right now, I'd still be short on sleep. Six hours…five…four. How will I get through the day with so little sleep? Yet working so hard to sleep just doesn't seem to work. Why is it so easy to fall asleep, to stay asleep, when it's almost time to get up? Merciful God, help me quiet my busy mind, and not work so hard at resting.

> *Come to me, all you that are weary and are carrying heavy burdens, and I will give you rest. Take my yoke upon you, and learn from me; for I am gentle and humble in heart, and you will find rest for your souls. For my yoke is easy, and my burden is light. (Matthew 11:28-29)*

MY PREYERS

Change and Changes

Sometimes people say they are too old to change. That's a sad statement. Some are too young to feel that way. Some are old enough to know better. Change can be difficult—for groups, for individuals. Groups face the challenge of preserving cherished traditions, while responding to changing times. Individuals face similar challenges in life, but making it harder still is the pressure of feeling alone. It's especially important during the watches of the night to remember that you are not alone, that God is always present. And that change is a part of life and growth and creation.

❀ Chosen Changes

It's not that I object to change, God. I know it's a part of life. It's the changes that are imposed from without, instead of by choice, that I have a hard time with. Well, all right, sometimes the ones I choose have unexpected consequences or complications too. But still, you know what I mean. God of Wisdom, help me to choose my changes wisely. And to respond with grace to the ones I do not choose.

> *God is our refuge and strength, a very present help in trouble. Therefore we will not fear, though the earth should change, though the mountains shake in the heart of the sea; though its waters roar and foam, though the mountains tremble with its tumult. (Psalm 46:1-3)*

❀ Transitions

O God, I thought that when I became a "grown up," my life, my feelings and thoughts would be so much more settled. Instead, I sometimes feel as if I'm in a permanent state of transition. Giver and Sustainer of Life, if this is the way it's going to be, could you give me some kind of clue or closure, so that I'll know that this is the way it's supposed to be...for now?

> *Your word is a lamp to my feet and a light to my path. (Psalm 119:105)*

❈ New Creation

Living things change. I know that; I see it in the garden year round. It changes with the time of day, with weekly weather, from season to season. Even stones, I have heard, change over great periods of time. Everything changes—except you, Eternal One, there before the beginning. God, help me to recognize that change is part of your ongoing process of creation. And help me to remember that I am a part of it too.

From now on, therefore, we regard no one from a human point of view; even though we once knew Christ from a human point of view, we know him no longer in that way. So if anyone is in Christ, there is a new creation: everything old has passed away; see, everything has become new! (2 Corinthians 5:16-17)

❈ Wind, Breath and Spirit

The winds of change are blowing yet again, God. I don't exactly know what's coming, but I feel it coming. I see it in the shifting, drifting clouds. I hear it in the rustling of the leaves. Wondrous God, with the winds of change, send the breath of your Spirit to bring new life.

The wind blows where it chooses, and you hear the sound of it, but you do not know where it comes from or where it goes. So it is with everyone who is born of the Spirit. (John 3:8).

MY PRAYERS

Children

When your children are babies, you learn to listen for cries in the night, cries that indicate some kind of need, even when your need is sleep. It goes with the territory. And in the long run, it's well worth it. They are your family. Sometimes, too, it's important to expand your notion of who "family" is. That isn't always easy either. And sometimes that child's voice in the night is your own.

✿ Yours, Mine and Ours

God, you invite us to call you Father. What an astonishing, amazing thing. That we, the whole unruly, worrisome lot of us, are your children. I wonder, God, do you weep with me when I weep, laugh with me when I laugh? Do you ever stay awake nights, years, millennia, eons, worrying about me, my safety, my happiness, my tomorrows and todays? Creator God, watch over all of your children, yours, mine and ours, each day, each night.

And I will be your father, and you shall be my sons and daughters,
says the Lord Almighty. (2 Corinthians 6:18)

✿ Other People's Children

Call me petty, God, but let me get it out: How is it that other people's children seem to go through life so easily, with things always going their way, when mine sometimes have to face such difficulties? Couldn't things go their way, too? And how is it, loving God, that other people's children sometimes have to face such terrible things, things such as wars and hunger, illness and oppression, neglect and poverty? Help me to remember one thing, Source of All Compassion: Just as I may love my children even more when times are hardest for them, so do you.

I will not leave you orphaned; I am coming to you. In a little while the world will
no longer see me, but you will see me; because I live, you also will live. On that
day you will know that I am in my Father, and you in me, and I in you.
(John 14:18-20)

❋ Stepparenting, or I Walk the Line

O God, it isn't always easy being a parent. You must know this well after eons of experience. And being a stepparent is a case by itself, a little like the hit song "I Walk the Line"—being enough of a parent without being too much of one. Seeing in your spouse's child not only another's child, but also the traits you love in your spouse. And I guess it isn't easy being a stepchild either. It takes a lot of accommodation, on both sides: child and grownup. Help us to grow in this together as we form our family—and yours.

Conduct yourselves wisely toward outsiders, making the most of the time. Let your speech always be gracious, seasoned with salt, so that you may know how you ought to answer everyone. (Colossians 4:5)

❋ Credit, Blame and Creation

Why is it, God, that whatever goes right for my children, I attribute it to them and/or to your grace, but whenever anything goes wrong for them, I immediately assume it's my fault as a parent? Is it just me? Or maybe it's just part of being a parent. Long after my children will stop being children, I'll never stop being a parent. And yet there can be astonishing job satisfaction in raising children. It would be a much different world without them. Did you look at humankind at the dawn of creation and think the same thing, Father/Mother God?

So God created humankind in his own image, in the image of God he created them; male and female he created them. (Genesis 1:27)

MY PRAYERS

Confusion

One of my children once said, with childhood innocence or insight, "This isn't my day. It must be somebody else's." I suspect you have had a few of those days yourself, or weeks or months. Times when chaos reigns, and when confusion seems to triumph over order. Like it or not, this is a part of life. Sometimes it just takes time to sort things out, to understand what they're about.

❀ At Sea

Jesus, my Brother, tonight I feel so storm-tossed and at sea, I'm uncertain where the shore is or how to get there. And furthermore, I suspect my boat has sprung a leak. You woke from the sleep of the weary to calm the storm and the disciples. Bringer of Peace and Stillness, bring them to my heart tonight.

> A great windstorm arose, and the waves beat into the boat, so that the boat was already being swamped. But he was in the stern, asleep on the cushion, and they woke him up and said to him, "Teacher, do you not care that we are perishing?" He woke up and rebuked the wind, and said to the sea, "Peace! Be still!" Then the wind ceased, and there was a dead calm. (Mark 4:37-39)

❀ Temptations/Tests

I don't like feeling this way, God, whatever this unwelcome, mixed up feeling is inside. And yet it would be too easy to act impulsively, to ignore integrity. It would be all too easy to silence that nagging little spoiled-sport voice that warns, "Slow down, you're getting it wrong." Someone of strong character is needed here. God, I think it will have to be you.

> No testing has overtaken you that is not common to everyone. God is faithful, and he will not let you be tested beyond your strength, but with the testing he will also provide the way out so that you may be able to endure it. (1 Corinthians 10:13)

❈ Sense and Song

How did life become so confused and so chaotic, God? Can you help me out of this mess, or at least help me make sense of it? I hope there is some point to all of this. I'm assuming there is. But right now, I surely don't see it. Or maybe I have to listen. Maybe I have to listen for the counterpoint harmony, not just what seems to be the melody. God of Hope, let me open my heart and ears to your song.

He drew me up from the desolate pit, out of the miry bog, and set my feet upon a rock, making my steps secure. He put a new song in my mouth, a song of praise to our God. (Psalm 40:2-3)

MY PRAYERS

Decisions

Think about this statement: "You can know the consequences only of decisions you actually make. You can't know the consequences of the 'other' decisions— the ones you might have made instead." (This includes, of course, *not* making a decision, which is a kind of decision in itself.) By deciding to do one thing differently, that "one thing" changes other things as well. Did you ever play the game "Pick-Up Sticks"? Remember how touching one stick could bring the whole thing down? Decision-making can be a scary proposition. When you find yourself in that valley of indecision, it's important to remember that you are not alone.

✤ Choices

O God, sometimes I feel as though I have too many choices. It's like a decision buffet. And sometimes it seems as if I have none at all. The buffet is closed. God of Wisdom, help me to seek and to find the right choices. For me. For you.

> *He has told you, O mortal, what is good; and what does the Lord require of you but to do justice, and to love kindness, and to walk humbly with your God? (Micah 6:8)*

✤ Really Big Decisions

Over and over I turn it around in my mind, God. Look at it this way and then that way. Decide to do this, decide to do that. How in the world am I supposed to decide what to do? God of Promise, could you give me a hint? Or at least let me know that you're there with me, while I try to figure out my path, your path, our path?

> *Multitudes, multitudes, in the valley of decision! For the day of the Lord is near in the valley of decision. (Joel 3:14)*

❦ Small Big Decisions

What am I going to do, God? Whatever am I going to do? Every decision I might make seems wrong, but then again, maybe right. God, I know that in the grand scheme of things it's a minor matter, nothing earthshaking. But I spend most of my time in the small scheme of things, so to me it does matter. Gracious God, I ask for some peace of mind, a sense of resolution. Not for a lifetime, just for these days...this night.

> *If any of you is lacking in wisdom, ask God, who gives to all generously and ungrudgingly, and it will be given you. (James 1:5)*

❦ The Sounds in Silence

Am I doing the right thing? In the spaces of the night, I wonder. I'm trying, God, but I could use a little help. What I need is a wisdom figure, a grown-up, to help me with this decision. Divine Teacher, I'm listening for your guidance. But all I hear is silence. Are you speaking too softly? Or am I not listening enough?

> *He said, "Go out and stand on the mountain before the Lord, for the Lord is about to pass by." Now there was a great wind, so strong that it was splitting mountains and breaking rocks in pieces before the Lord, but the Lord was not in the wind; and after the wind an earthquake, but the Lord was not in the earthquake; and after the earthquake a fire, but the Lord was not in the fire; and after the fire a sound of sheer silence. When Elijah heard it, he wrapped his face in his mantle and went out and stood at the entrance of the cave. (1 Kings 19:11-13)*

MY PRAYERS

Discouragement and the Dark Hours

I read somewhere that, in the depths of winter, bison face into the north wind. I don't know if this is true or not, but during times of difficulty, I picture myself as one of them, head down, facing into the wind. Surviving. Does this image resonate with you?

❄ Winter Winds

O God, the winds of loss and change are blowing hard. I stand here, head lowered, at the edge of the herd, facing into the winds of winter. Cold winds and blowing snow make it difficult to see ahead. Spring and warmth, green grass and shoots seem far away, a dream only vaguely recalled in this winter darkness. Be with me, Holy Comforter, in this time of survival. And now and then, send in the wind a faint hint or whiff of warmth and greening, to remind me that spring is more than a dream.

> *Arise, my love, my fair one, and come away. For now the winter is past, the rain is over and gone. The flowers appear upon the earth; the time of singing has come, and the voice of the turtledove is heard in our land. The fig tree puts forth its figs, and the vines are in blossom; they give forth fragrance. Arise, my love, my fair one, and come away. (Song of Solomon 2:10-13)*

❄ Coping and Courage

O God of Understanding, I don't know how I will cope with what is happening. I just don't think I'm up to this situation, this task. I don't know how to handle it. But there aren't any alternatives to coping, one way or another. All I can do is say to myself, "Have courage. Have courage." And reach for your hand.

> *Keep alert, stand firm in your faith, be courageous, be strong. Let all that you do be done in love. (1 Corinthians 16:13-14)*

❈ Leading Through

Lord Jesus, you endured the worst of pain, of suffering, in the midst of rejection and humiliation. You endured an awful trial in your lifetime and came through on the other side, so I can't say you don't know how I feel. You do. Be with me now, Risen Lord, in this time, in this place, and lead me through.

Even though I walk through the darkest valley, I fear no evil; for you are with me; your rod and your staff—they comfort me. (Psalm 23:4)

MY PRAYERS

Faith and Doubts

By definition, if you know something for certain, and can prove it beyond a reasonable doubt, you don't have to have faith. Faith is a leap *beyond* pure reason. It isn't *un*reasonable. It just goes beyond reason. So while absolute proof may eliminate faith, doubt does not—fortunately. Maybe it's just a part of the whole thing. If you don't believe in something, you don't have something to doubt. And anyway, doubters can be in good company. Remember Job? And Peter? And Thomas?

✤ Night Skies and Hidden Stars

God, I remember learning about your stars flung prodigally across the sky: celebrity stars such as the Pole star and Sirius, constellations such as the Big Dipper and the Lady Cassiopeia, and all those ordinary, lovely stars whose names few know. But now, too often, lights and haze pale their brilliance, or I'm too busy to look up and take notice. But they're still there, all those stars, even if I can't see them. And you're still there, too, aren't you, God of Heaven and Earth, even if it's sometimes hard to see your presence, hidden for the moment by haze and hurry?

> *Can you bind the chains of the Pleiades, or loose the cords of Orion? Can you lead forth the Mazzaroth in their season, or can you guide the Bear with its children? Do you know the ordinances of the heavens? Can you establish their rule on the earth? (Job 38:31-33)*

❈ Other People's Paths

God of All, help me to remember my other brothers and sisters, your other children, of other faiths, of little faith, or of no faith. And help us all to grow in you, even when we grow without knowing. Hold them, hold me, in your loving hands.

> *I am the good shepherd. I know my own and my own know me, just as the Father knows me and I know the Father. And I lay down my life for the sheep. I have other sheep that do not belong to this fold. I must bring them also, and they will listen to my voice. So there will be one flock, one shepherd. (John 10:14-16)*

❈ Insights

Lord Jesus, sometimes I don't know where I fit into your flock. I'm drawn to this insight and that, this idea and that, sampling a taste here, a taste there, at the great buffet of belief and ideas. Who can know all the paths that lead to you? And yet, what I can know is this: Without you, Jesus, who walked the earth, who felt joy and sorrow and disappointment and hope, who gave love and who was loved, my life would be bleak indeed, in good times as well as bad. I know that it is through you that I can glimpse the vast mystery behind you. It's still quite astonishing that you—you!—would choose to share the human condition.

> *Long ago God spoke to our ancestors in many and various ways by the prophets, but in these last days he has spoken to us by a Son, whom he has appointed heir of all things, through whom he also created the worlds. He is the reflection of God's glory and the exact imprint of God's very being, and he sustains all things by his powerful word. (Hebrews 1:1-3)*

MY PRAYERS

Forgiveness

When my mother was alive, she used to say, "You can be big enough to build bridges, Helen Irene." Mothers sometimes overestimate us, even when they're right. Sometimes building bridges is an important part of mutual forgiveness. There are other times when forgiveness seems foolish, maybe even heroic, or at least out of reach. Sometimes forgiveness is simply letting go. However legitimate, carrying a grudge is very much BYOB: "Bring Your Own Burden." The longer and further you carry it, the heavier it gets and the more energy it takes—energy that could be channeled into other uses and freed for greater things.

❄ Forgive and Remember

I haven't found many hard-to-forgive people in my lifetime, God. But there have been a few. Real harm was done. And to make matters worse, the harm was intentional, or at least the consequences didn't seem to matter to the offender. God of Mercy, help me to hold your example of forgiveness in my heart—all the forgiveness I've needed and received. Help me also to remember that it is forgiving, as well as forgiveness, that sets me free.

> *As God's chosen ones, holy and beloved, clothe yourselves with compassion, kindness, humility, meekness, and patience. Bear with one another and, if anyone has a complaint against another, forgive each other; just as the Lord has forgiven you, so you must also forgive. Above all, clothe yourselves with love, which binds everything together in perfect harmony. (Colossians 3:12-14)*

❇ Knowing When to Say When

God of Righteousness, I know well that I'm not always right, and sometimes I'm really wrong. You know it well, too. And I know that there are times when "who's right" and "who's wrong" don't really matter. But, God, where do I stand on those bridges when I'm with someone who thinks they're always right and never really wrong? Help me to know when and how to stand my ground when I should and not fall into the trap of thinking or needing to be always right myself.

Have nothing to do with stupid and senseless controversies; you know that they breed quarrels. (2 Timothy 2:23)

❇ Hard Forgiveness

Loving God, it is really hard to forgive this person. This is someone who should have known better. Anyone should have known better, Oh, yes, *now* this person is sorry. But isn't it a little late? I don't see how things can be undone, either. I know that I am supposed to be forgiving, just as you are forgiving. But in this case it's so hard. Especially because the person who caused the pain is me.

For day and night your hand was heavy upon me; my strength was dried up as by the heat of summer. Then I acknowledged my sin to you, and I did not hide my iniquity; I said "I will confess my transgressions to the Lord," and you forgave the guilt of my sin. (Psalm 32:4-5)

MY PREYERS

Friends in High Places

One of the difficulties in being an insomniac is that it can be lonely on the night watch—being awake when it seems that everyone else is sleeping. Few friends are going to welcome a chatty call at 2:00 a.m.—with one exception. It can seem a little strange, at times, to think of the God of Mystery, Creator of the Universe and awaited Redeemer, among other job titles, as a friend. Here is a being who is perfectly willing to take your calls, no matter the time, no matter how often. Here is someone who listens attentively, and who speaks, if you can catch it, with love, wisdom and universal concern—a true friend indeed.

❋ Night Music

"It's a quarter to three. There's no one in the place, except you and me." So begins "One For My Baby," a Johnny Mercer song made popular by Frank Sinatra a lifetime ago. But I feel as if it's my song too. It seems to me, God, that being awake during the day is enough. Why should I need to be awake at night besides? I'm not getting my fair share of sleep. Why is that? Isn't there enough to go around? I know that there are a lot of us out there—awake, that is. But at "a quarter to three," it seems as if it's only thee and me. On the other hand, dear friend, could I ask for better company?

> *I do not call you servants any longer, because the servant does not know what his master is doing; but I have called you friends, because I have made known to you everything that I have heard from my Father. (John 15:15)*

❇ As One Would Speak to a Friend

Is it all right, God, to use this time for prayer? I sometimes feel a little strange about this late-night praying. It feels so casual; flat on my back or propped up with pillows in bed, conversing in the night like a sleepover with friends. Should I make an appointment? Shouldn't I drag myself out of bed so I can at least be more uncomfortable? During the day, I often don't manage to find time for you. At night, when my options narrow, I do. So now you're my new best friend. Of course, you were always willing to be. Help me look at the next fifteen minutes, the next half-hour, as a gift, as uninterrupted time with a friend.

> *Thus the Lord used to speak to Moses face to face, as one speaks to a friend. (Exodus 33:11)*

❇ Up Close (or Maybe Not) and Personal

One of the good things about trying to talk with you, God, is that I can come to you just as I am. Since you already know what I'm like—good, bad and sometimes uncertain which is which—I don't have to watch my words. I don't have to worry about being false or making a good impression. You already know me better than that. Nor do I have to worry that, if you know what I'm really like, you won't love me any more. You already know the real me.

> *O Lord, you have searched me and known me. You know when I sit down and when I rise up; you discern my thoughts from far away. You search out my path and my lying down, and are acquainted with all my ways. (Psalm 139:1-3)*

MY PREMA... MY PRAYERS

_____

_____

_____

_____

_____

_____

Friends in Low Places

You can never know exactly how someone else feels. But you can know when someone you love—friend or family—is hurting. Even when it is someone you don't know, there are still ways to be a friend. It can be hard to know what to do or say. Sometimes the only thing you can do is to say, "I'm so sorry," and try to figure out what you'd like someone else to do if it were you.

❈ Friends Finding Their Way

Dear God, some of my friends are going through very hard times in their lives right now, and I just don't know how to help. And sometimes I get too caught up in my life to help as much as I could, and probably should. Maybe I could at least offer an understanding heart, a listening ear, and a closed mouth. God of Sorrows, be with them as their friend to comfort and guide. And, God, when I'm in one of those low places, help me to be a friend to myself.

Blessed be the God and Father of our Lord Jesus Christ, the Father of mercies and the God of all consolation, who consoles us in all our affliction, so that we may be able to console those who are in any affliction with the consolation with which we ourselves are consoled by God. (2 Corinthians 1:3-4)

❈ Advice

I know people mean well, God, but sometimes I don't need to add unsolicited advice to the burden I'm already carrying. Help me to consider their advice honestly, discern what is right for me, and tactfully ignore what is not. And then, help me move ahead and do it your way and my way. And when I'm inclined to offer advice, let me remember how this feels, so that I don't make matters worse. Discerning God, help me to help others wisely, to offer words when words should be offered, to withhold them when they should not, and above all, to listen with an understanding heart.

Rash words are like sword thrusts, but the tongue of the wise brings healing. (Proverbs 12:18)

Unsaid Prayers for Unshed Tears/Forget-Them-Nots

For all the people for whom I said I would pray, for the ones I remembered and the ones I forgot; for all those who have need of being remembered and know it, and for those who do not; for those who don't believe in prayer and wish they did; for those who believe but are in pain and cannot pray; for all who have no one to pray for, and no one to pray for them; for all those for whom I'd pray if I could; even, with your help, Loving God, for those for whom I'd rather not pray...for all them and for me, be present through this night and through the coming tomorrows.

> *Now may our Lord Jesus Christ himself and God our Father, who loved us and through grace gave us eternal comfort and good hope, comfort your hearts and strengthen them in every good work and word. (2 Thessalonians 2:16)*

MY PRAYERS

Gifts and Grace

Saint Paul, in various metaphors—particularly in the beautiful imagery of the body of Christ in Chapter 12 of First Corinthians—tells us that we each have different gifts to contribute. Preachers and spiritual writers have built on this idea ever since. The idea is at once awesome and comforting. Putting it into practice can be a challenge. How well do you know—and use—your gifts?

❋ Empty Hands

Eternal Friend, you know I'm learning to like talking with you—and, better yet, listening to you. But I also don't want to come empty-handed and not give anything back. So how do I hold up my end of this friendship? Here's the question I keep asking: "What is it that is special about me?" I'm not asking for flattery here, God, just for information. What are my gifts, and how do you want me to use my gifts—and my weaknesses? How can I help in the work of your hands? And please, God, let it be something I can handle!

Now there are varieties of gifts, but the same Spirit; and there are varieties of services, but the same Lord; and there are varieties of activities, but it is the same God who activates all of them in everyone. To each is given the manifestation of the Spirit for the common good. (1 Corinthians 12:4-7)

❀ Goodness Grace-ious

God of Mystery, there was a time when I couldn't have imagined talking with you this way—friend to friend—because, basically, I figured you didn't like me. How could you? I just couldn't get it right. If I wasn't doing something I shouldn't, I was failing to do something I should. Furthermore, even if I were an improved me—a vastly improved me—how could I approach a supreme being whom I could never begin to truly comprehend? And then I began to get it. That's what grace does. It brings you to me and me to you.

> *Three times I appealed to the Lord about this, that it would leave me, but he said to me, "My grace is sufficient for you, for power is made perfect in weakness." So, I will boast all the more gladly of my weakness, so that the power of Christ may dwell in me. (2 Corinthians 12:8-9)*

❀ Multiple Choice/One Size Does Not Fit All

Here I am again, God, talking about those gifts. Some people are called to big things, but I strongly suspect I'm called more to medium-sized things. And maybe that's a relief. It's not that I don't want to use my gifts to serve you, God-Who-Calls. I just don't know how they fit in. Do I have to do things I don't like doing? Or can I do things I actually like to do? Do I need to learn to do things I can't do already? Or am I already using my gifts but taking them for granted? Maybe it's all of the above. I think I'll just have to keep looking and listening for the answers. And in the meantime, tomorrow I'll work on doing some of those medium-sized things.

> *With what shall I come before the Lord, and bow myself before God on high? (Micah 6:6)*

MY PRAYERS

_____

_____

_____

_____

_____

Gratitude and Joyful Noise

Most of us are quite restrained in our spiritual expressions of thanks. But scripture records others who weren't so inhibited: King David "danced before the ark with all his might" (2 Samuel 6:14); the psalmists called for music and shouts of joy. Maybe getting up to dance in the middle of the night is not an option for you, and shouting and stringed instruments might annoy the neighbors. But you can still have a song in your heart and a smile on your lips, even in darkness, and in the morning, maybe, just for a moment, your own song and dance.

❀ Joy

God, tonight I can't sleep because I'm happy. something really great happened. What a ridiculous and wonderful reason for staying awake. To tell the truth, though, I'd rather be asleep at the moment and save the wide-awake joy for morning. But still, what a ridiculous and wonderful reason for being awake. Thanks, My Friend!

> *Praise him with trumpet sound; praise him with lute and harp! Praise him with tambourine and dance; praise him with strings and pipe! Praise him with clanging cymbals; praise him with loud clashing cymbals! Let everything that breathes praise the Lord! (Psalm 150:4-6)*

❀ Laughter

Thank you, Joyful God, for the gift of laughter. Not unkind laughter at others, surely, but good-natured, heart-felt chuckles at life and at myself. Let me remember with a light heart the times of laughter, hold onto humor at times when I need it most, and share joy when I can. And when I pass on, Dear God, let me be remembered with laughter, too.

> *Then our mouth was filled laughter, and our tongue with shouts of joy; then it was said among the nations, "The Lord has done great things for them." (Psalm 126:2)*

Timing

God, you did it again. Thank you. Once again you saved me from doing or saying something really foolish or petty—just in the nick of time. It was a close call. It often is, isn't it? But once again, God of Understanding, I have to thank you for saving me—from myself.

Even before a word is on my tongue, O Lord, you know it completely. You hem me in, behind and before, and lay your hand upon me. (Psalm 139:4-5)

Rain and Rhythms

I love the sound of a gentle rain at night, God. I love to listen the rhythm of the rain, to watch the drops slide down the windowpane. Sometimes, surprisingly, I even try to stay awake to watch and listen. It soothes my soul and refreshes your Earth and signals your presence. God of All Creation, for gentle rain I thank you. And in seasons of dryness, let me look and listen for the rhythms of your work.

Ask rain from the Lord in the season of the spring rain, from the Lord who makes the storm clouds, who gives showers of rain to you, the vegetation in the field to everyone. (Zechariah 10:1)

MY PRAYERS

Growing Old-er Without Growing Old

The late, great Bette Davis once said, in her unforgettable voice, "Growing old is not for sissies." Probably not. But it's also important to remember that a lot of people never get the opportunity to prove a particular type of courage by growing old. So, stand—or sit—proud and seize the years.

❈ (Un?)Favorable Rate of Exchange

Sometimes, My Eternal Friend, I feel that with the passage of time so much is being stripped bare. Little by little, gradually or suddenly, bits and pieces are drifting away. Family and friends move to another part of my world; or further away, to a part of yours. Career options changed vastly before I even decided what I wanted to be when I grew up. Some things that I could once do so easily are a little, or lot, more difficult, and sometimes not do-able at all. And when I look in the mirror, God, is that rather distinguished-looking, rather *mature*-appearing person, still me? Where did my other face go? Hold me in the refuge of your love.

> *I will repay you for the years that the swarming locust has eaten, the hopper, the destroyer, and the cutter, my great army, which I sent against you. You shall eat in plenty and be satisfied, and praise the name of the Lord your God, who has dealt wondrously with you. And my people shall never again be put to shame. (Joel 2:25-26)*

❈ Too Old to Dream?

God, there's an old song that begins, "When I grow too old to dream…" It's a lovely song about memories. Oh, I cherish my memories. But please, God of Hope, never let me grow too old to dream.

> *Then afterward I will pour out my spirit on all flesh; your sons and your daughters shall prophesy, your old men shall dream dreams, and your young men shall see visions. (Joel 2:28)*

✵ Growing Pains

God of Small Things, sometimes I have to sit back and remind myself that everything in your loving world takes time to become itself and flourish. The acorn that is merely food for foragers becomes that glorious oak. Butterflies start from a chrysalis. Oysters form pearls by getting irritated. Grape juice and sugar do not become good wine overnight. So let me remember to be grateful for the time to become who I am meant to be.

In old age they still produce fruit; they are always green and full of sap, showing that the Lord is upright; he is my rock, and there is no unrighteousness in him. (Psalm 92:14-15)

✵ Gratitude—Sometimes

I don't want to sound like a Pollyanna, which is an old reference in itself, God, but as I grow older, there are some advantages I have to admit. For example, I can now say "no" without feeling pressure or guilt. Well, not too much anyway. I've acquired a certain amount of wisdom that is useful to me and that, now and then, someone actually wants. I no longer worry about making an impression; it's already been made. For good or ill. There's a certain pride in knowing that I've made it this far on the journey, detours, train changes, mislaid maps, and all. Help me remember that I'm not just growing older; I'm growing up—and I'm going somewhere.

Do not remember the former things, or consider the things of old. I am about to do a new thing; now it springs forth, do you not perceive it? I will make a way in the wilderness and rivers in the desert. (Isaiah 43:18-19)

MY PRAYERS

Hearth, Heart and Home

The word "home" is freighted with meaning. It is sometimes used interchangeably with house, but has significance far beyond it. It has been said that home is where the heart is. Nomadic peoples carried their homes with them. Poet Robert Frost said, "Home is the place where, when you have to go there, they have to take you in." At the beginning of Chapter 14 in John's Gospel, Jesus spoke of going home. Home is one of the most basic of human needs: Here or there; now, or then.

Nowhere a Bed

Somewhere, God, people are traveling, willingly or unwillingly. Somewhere, people are working, some are even playing. And somewhere, somewhere, a lot of people are sleeping. But not me. Me, I lay here in bed, ready for sleep, the invited guest that doesn't show up for the party. But of even more consequence, somewhere there are people without a bed, without a roof, without a place to lay their head. Compassionate God, help me to be awake to their needs.

And Jesus said to him, "Foxes have holes and the birds of the air have nests; but the Son of Man has nowhere to lay his head." (Matthew 8:20)

The Neighborhood

Creator God, you have provided a perfectly gorgeous planet on which to live—air, water, mountains, valleys, deserts, rivers, forests, cities new and old. And that doesn't even count the stars, the sun and moon and other planets. (As nice as this one? Well, maybe. But I'm still fond of this neighborhood.) Breath of Life, help me to use and share your Earth's resources with wisdom, justice and generosity.

You crown the year with your bounty; your wagon tracks overflow with richness. The pastures of the wilderness overflow, the hills gird themselves with joy, the meadows clothe themselves with flocks, the valleys deck themselves with grain, they shout and sing together for joy. (Psalm 65:11-13)

❈ Homesick

O God, I'm a grownup. I'm not supposed to be homesick, especially when I'm at home. But I want some parts of my past to come back, a time when home was different, or felt different. I want some of the people who passed through to come back. I even want some parts of myself to come back—although not all of them. Some are better left behind. But I'm also learning that wherever I am, Dear Comforter, you are with me. And that means I'm home.

By the rivers of Babylon—there we sat down and there we wept
when we remembered Zion. (Psalm 137:1)

❈ Homes

Thank you, Gracious God, for all of the homes and hearts that have welcomed me over the years, decades and lifetimes—for those I appreciated then; for those I appreciate only now. God, this night can we send them blessings to flow come morning? Help me, too, to have a welcoming heart, as I have been welcomed by you.

Welcome one another, therefore, just as Christ has welcomed you,
for the glory of God. (Romans 15:7)

MY PRAYERS

Holidays and Hallowed Days

Holidays are supposed to be wonderful. They *can* be wonderful. But they can also be difficult. And some special days are not holidays at all, just special in their own ways. These might best be called hallowed days.

✖ Holy Week

Risen Lord, do you ever relive those last terrible days of your life on this earth? The days before the wonderful surprise—to most people anyway—ending? Sometimes I wish I could have been there with you, so you wouldn't have been so alone. You who were there with all of us, past, present and future, even if we helped put you there. But I'm afraid that I would have been just as frightened as everyone else and kept my distance. So, to be truthful, Lord, I guess I'm glad I wasn't there. But still, I wonder what it felt like—a few days or weeks later—to run home swiftly, with joy, to say: "You'll never believe it. I still can hardly believe it. Guess who I saw and spoke with today."

> *That same hour they got up and returned to Jerusalem; and they found the eleven and their companions gathered together. They were saying, "The Lord has risen indeed, and he has appeared to Simon!" Then they told what had happened on the road, and how he had been made known to them in the breaking of the bread. (Luke 24:33-35)*

✖ Deck the Halls

Holidays can sometimes be hard, God. So much has changed from the holidays I remember—the magical Christmases of my childhood, the Easters with young children (did we ever find all those eggs?), not to mention unjustly ignored Pentecost. And all the others, the in-between holidays. Your feasts have seen lots of changes, too, God. From people to people, place to place, over a few thousand years. Help me remember their meaning: birth, death, new life, New Creation, Spirit. Maybe a sign should be posted: "Silence or singing, please. God at work."

The Lord spoke to Moses, saying, "Speak to the people of Israel and say to them: These are the appointed festivals of the Lord that you shall proclaim as holy convocations, my appointed festivals." (Leviticus 23:1-2)

✳ Ordinary Times

Thank you, ever-present God, for an ordinary day full of ordinary things. Nothing dramatic. Nothing really exciting. Just ordinary joys, work and concerns. For this, I am truly grateful. And, God, help those who long for ordinary days.

First of all, then, I urge that supplications, prayer, intercessions, and thanksgivings be made for everyone, for kings and all who are in high positions, so that we may lead a quiet and peaceable life, in all godliness and dignity. (1 Timothy 2:1-2)

✳ Birthdays, Baptisms and Beginnings

God of Beginnings, tomorrow is the anniversary of my birth, or of my baptism, or of whatever anniversary I need. My personal New Year's Eve, without having to stay awake until midnight. (Except that I'm already awake.) For these moments—for these hours, maybe—it is my time. A time of promise. And "Beginnings" with a capital B. Even if I've already had a lot of Birthdays, and Beginnings, and promises fulfilled and unfulfilled. Even so—especially so—God, always keep alive in me a sense of beginnings.

And the one who was seated on the throne said, "See, I am making all things new." (Revelation 21:5)

MY PRAYERS

Illness

When you're sick, it's not easy to think of other people, to feel connected. My mother used to tell me that when my father was in the hospital after a major heart attack, he prayed for the patients he could hear moaning in the night. Illness can isolate people. It can imprison body, mind, even spirit—*can*, not *does*. No two illnesses are alike, not even when they are the same illness. Illness is as individual as the person who is ill. When you're sick, you experience illness differently, suffer differently, cope differently, seek healing differently than any other person. You bring the unique person you are to your illness.

❊ Compassion by Night

Compassionate God, as I lie here awake, I think of the many others who are lying awake, at this very minute—in hospitals, in nursing homes, in care facilities—who are also in pain. If I could hear their moaning, would I pray for them? Or would I wish they would just be quiet so I might sleep? God, help me to have compassion, even as I need compassion. And especially be with all those who suffer illness, with all those who moan, even silently, in the night.

> *Out of the depths I cry to you, O Lord. Lord, hear my voice! Let your ears be attentive to the voice of my supplications! (Psalm 130:1-2)*

❊ Fourth Opinions

I know people are well-intentioned, Lord Jesus, when they speak to me of sure-fire cures, pain relievers and other remedies tried so successfully by friends of friends. Sometimes they may even be right and helpful. But you, my Brother, have walked the path. You know that I need to walk my own path, make my own journey. Lord, help other people to remember that, when it comes to sickness, one size does not fit all. And help me to remember it, too.

> *Who is this that darkens counsel by words without knowledge? (Job 38:2)*

Seasons

"For everything there is a season…a time to sleep and a time to wake." No, wait. It doesn't say that, but maybe it should. Morning is a time for waking. This is supposed to be a time for sleep. Not planting or plucking, or losing or keeping, or gathering or healing. No, wait. It does say that. It's always a season for healing, whether of body, mind or spirit. Faithful God, who is with me through all seasons, be with me and with all who need healing this night.

> *For everything there is a season, and a time for every matter under heaven: a time to be born, and a time to die; a time to plant, and a time to pluck up what is planted; a time to kill, and a time to heal; a time to break down, and a time to build up…a time to seek, and a time to lose; a time to keep, and a time to throw away. (Ecclesiastes 3:1-3, 6)*

MY PRAYERS

Journeys

For most of my life, part of the sounds of night have been the sounds of journey: the clunk-clunk of tire chains on a snowy, small street in my childhood town; the sound of a train whistle echoing across the countryside; the rumble of the elevated train a block to the east in the city where I now live; the distant drone of night flights overhead on the glide path to and from the airport. There's a certain magic in the idea of journey. The lure of adventure, the unknown, the challenge. The call to be on the way *somewhere*. It's a small wonder that spiritual writers speak of journey as theme. You are on your own personal journey, on your way. Where are you headed tonight?

✻ Counting Lost Sheep

I think I misread the map, Lord, or forgot to read it altogether. Sometimes I wonder where and how I fit in your fold. If I were to count sheep for sleeping, I would have to start with the lost, strayed and blundering ones, the ones that fall in ravines and streams and have to be pulled out. Then I would move on to the ones that can't recognize a wolf in sheep's clothing. And how could I forget the ones that hear your voice and come running, but get distracted along the way. Lord Jesus, when we lose each other, please remember to come back for me.

> So he told them this parable: "Which one of you, having a hundred sheep and losing one of them, does not leave the ninety-nine in the wilderness and go after the one that is lost until he finds it? When he has found it, he lays it on his shoulders and rejoices." (Luke 15:3-5)

❈ Oases and Outcroppings

I can't say, God, that I'm over the mountains, out of the desert and into the valley. Those mountains are high. There are rushing rivers to cross. And this can be one big, dry desert. But in the midst of this place, this journey, along the way I find sheltered outcroppings where I can rest, oases where I can be refreshed. And bridges. My strength and my salvation, for these unexpected places, I give you thanks.

> *A voice cries out:"In the wilderness prepare the way of the Lord, make straight in the desert a highway for our God. Every valley shall be lifted up, and every mountain and hill be made low; the uneven ground shall become level, and the rough places a plain."(Isaiah 40:3-4)*

❈ Flying into the Dawn

High above, I hear planes on their glide path. I wonder where they're going this night. Surely some are making their way east, across the ocean, into the dawn. One moment there is only the vast, cold darkness outside the cabin window. And then, that first glimmer of light. Then more. Pink and gold and shimmering clouds. I imagine people beginning to stir in their cramped seats, getting a glimpse of land breaking through the clouds ahead. The long night of darkness—and some discomfort—is coming to an end, and suddenly it is morning, a new place, a new day. I wonder, sometimes, Awesome God, if that is what my last journey will be like: flying out of darkness, flying into your dawn.

> *Arise, shine, for your light has come, and the glory of the Lord has risen upon you. For darkness shall cover the earth, and thick darkness the peoples; but the Lord will arise upon you, and his glory will appear over you. (Isaiah 60:1-2)*

MY PRAYERS

Just As I Am

Sometimes it can be harder to admit to the small, petty sins than confess to the bigger ones. There might even be a certain dignity in sincerely acknowledging that you are a sinner. But it's tough to acknowledge to yourself, let alone anyone else, that you have *petty* thoughts. Yet, those same unwelcome thoughts can be the beginning of prayer, even in the middle of the night, or maybe *especially* in the middle of the night. There's no one else awake to talk to about them. And you probably wouldn't anyway. Why would you want to put that petty part of yourself on display? Except that God already knows; your thoughts are not breaking news. So they become part of the conversation in the watches of the night.

❊ Petty Thieves

One of the things I dislike most about being awake at night, God, is that it makes it easier for all those really petty thoughts to break in. Pettiness, pickiness, irritability, envy, jealousy, superiority, inferiority, the ones I'm embarrassed to have anyone but you know about. By day, it can be harder for them to enter—they don't so much like daylight. But come the night hours and, before you know it, they can break and enter under cover of darkness. Saving Presence, help me to guard the house of my soul.

> *Do not worry about anything, but in everything by prayer and supplication with thanksgiving let your requests be made known to God. And the peace of God, which surpasses all understanding, will guard your hearts and minds in Christ Jesus. (Philippians 4:6-7)*

✿ Fool's Paradise

It's bad enough, Lord, when things go wrong in spite of me. It's worse when I feel I've inadvertently given things a good shove in that direction. I really don't think I'm a fool, but there are days—and nights—when I feel like one. Lord Jesus, you came as both Servant and King. And I guess every king needs a jester. Lord, give me wisdom when needed. And when I lack it, at least let me be your fool.

> *All this I have tested by wisdom; I said, "I will be wise," but it was far from me. That which is, is far off, and deep, very deep; who can find it out? (Ecclesiastes 7:23-24)*

✿ Old Acquaintance

I have said it before, God, and I'll say it again, because it never ceases to surprise me: You know me so well and love me anyway. What a reassuring and redemptive thing to know! There's you, the God of Majesty and Mystery, Creator, Redeemer and Sustainer—and who knows what else in your spare time. And then there's me. It seems like such an unlikely combination. And yet knowing me and my faults—all of them, past and present—as well as you do, you still invite me into your presence. What can I say, patient God, except, here I am. Again.

> *When I look at the heavens, the work of your fingers, the moon and the stars that you have established; what are human beings that you are mindful of them, mortals that you care for them? Yet you have made them a little lower than God and crowned them with glory and honor. (Psalm 8:3-5)*

MY PRAYERS

_____

_____

_____

_____

_____

Learning Curves

I am the Leftover Queen. It's *not* true, as my children have suggested, that I recycled the original family meal, with added ingredients, for ten years. A week, maybe. But it is true that I don't like to waste things—not food, not experiences, good or bad. I think that if I have to go through them, I should be able to do something with them. Like recycle them and add a question: "What can I learn from all this?" It's not a bad question, you know. Try it out tonight.

❊ The Question

God, there was a time when I used to fret and stew when things went wrong— as you know, as my family and friends know, as probably my pets know. I still fret and stew some, but I also remember the question: What—and how—can I learn from this?

> *Did you experience so much for nothing?—if it really was for nothing.*
> *(Galatians 3:4)*

❊ Reduce Speed: Learning Curve Ahead

Some people are quick learners, God. Not me. I think I am one of those life-long ones. Not necessarily slow, just life-long. It either takes me multiple lessons before I catch the point, or I get it quickly, but I can't seem to apply it to the next lesson. Or it comes in a burst of insight, like the dawn that fades into night sky with the sunset, to await the next time things dawn. God of Surprises, help me to keep my mind and heart open.

> *I will instruct you and teach you the way you should go;*
> *I will counsel you with my eye upon you. (Psalm 32:8)*

Night School

Dear God, what am I supposed to learn from being awake so many nights? I assume I'm supposed to learn *something*. I mean, if I don't, it seems like such a waste. Persistent God, help me to remember that this night school is an extended opportunity for you to teach and for me to learn.

> *I will give you the treasures of darkness and riches hidden in secret places, so that you may know that it is I, the Lord, the God of Israel, who call you by your name. (Isaiah 45:3)*

MY PRAYERS

Letting Go

There is a popular saying that frequently appears on various media: "Let go and let God." It's thoughtful and thought-provoking, but it isn't always easy to do. Thoughts, feelings, habits and objects can be hard to put away. And sometimes it can be hard to decide what to discard. What is fundamental to your "interior home" and what is just clutter? Once you decide, you need to act on it. The prize comes in discovering what you want to make room for in your days, your heart, your mind and your life.

❊ Excess Baggage

God, on the occasions when I travel, I've learned to travel light so that the trip isn't for my luggage. What doesn't fit, doesn't go. So why can't I apply the same standards to the excess baggage I tend to carry around in my life? Old annoyances, unused dreams, over-commitments. Gracious Provider, help me to learn to travel light on my journey with you, and to carry only what is needed, what is helpful, and what fits.

> *He said to them, "Take nothing for your journey, no staff, nor bag, nor bread, nor money—not even an extra tunic. Whatever house you enter, stay there, and leave from there." (Luke 9:3-4)*

❊ Carping Diem

Carp, carp, carp. There I go again, God. Not gossip—deadly gossip is easy enough to avoid—but just plain carping about the world at large and about my little world. God, I don't suppose I'll ever seize the day to give up carping completely. But if I'm going to swim with the fishes, let me learn how and when to just enjoy the freedom of going with the flow. And while we're at it, Eternal Friend, let me learn also when to be a clam.

> *A fool takes no pleasure in understanding,*
> *but only in expressing personal opinion. (Proverbs 18:2)*

❊ Obstacles

Help me, God, to let go of the things that stand in the way of following your way, things that block me, things that weight me down, things that trip me up. But first, Holy God, help me recognize which things they are.

Set up road markers for yourself, make yourself signposts,
consider well the highway, the road by which you went. (Jeremiah 31:21)

MY PRAYERS

Loss and Sorrow

Faith doesn't take away the pain of loss and sorrow. It can't. But faith can and does give loss a different meaning. Faith can and does offer hope. When you are on the path of sorrow, faith offers the comfort that you are not alone. Faith points beyond life, beyond death, to what cannot be described or defined; to what can only be awaited, and walked toward, with wonder.

❀ Do You Know Who I Am?

How can I pray, God, when I am so filled with sorrow that I can't find room for anything else? I feel so alone and so bereft. How do I get through this night and the silence, usually such a welcome sound of peace, but now so empty? Can anyone know how I feel? Do you know, Breath of My Life? Do you care? With everything you have to attend to, all those people, creatures, worlds, do you remember me? Do you know who I am?

> *Do not fear, for I have redeemed you; I have called you by name, you are mine. When you pass through the waters, I will be with you; and through the rivers, they shall not overwhelm you; when you walk through fire you shall not be burned, and the flame shall not consume you. (Isaiah 43:1-2)*

❀ Creatures That Comfort

God, this week I lost an animal friend to the approach of death. Yes, I know some humans may say or think, "At least it's not a person." While they are right, it was still an important member of my family—a source of playfulness, comfort and fidelity, and unquestioning, unquenchable love. If only my heart could be that big. God of all things bright and beautiful, all creatures great and small, let Saint Francis, friend of creation, hold out loving arms to my animal friend.

> *Oh Lord, how manifold are your works! In wisdom you have made them all; the earth is full of your creatures. (Psalm 104:24)*

❀ Remembering Things Past

Sometimes when I close my eyes, God, I can bring back for a moment the world I used to live in, before such pain, such loss. Was that life really mine? Why did I take it for granted? Why didn't I appreciate it more? I would be so much wiser now if I had. Wisdom comes late, loving God. Let me now appreciate these days and these nights.

> *See, now is the acceptable time; see, now is the day of salvation!*
> *(2 Corinthians 6:2)*

❀ Dreams

Sometimes, not often, not nearly often enough, God-Beyond-Me, I dream of those I have lost to Death and Life. And for that brief dream moment, I can see them, speak to them and listen to them one more time. Maybe dreams are a form of Time Travel where, for just that moment, I can travel back days, months, years to a time when we were together. Or are dreams, instead, Time Travel forward to an unknown time when we will be together again?

> *If for this life only we have hoped in Christ, we are of all people most to be pitied.*
> *But in fact Christ has been raised from the dead, the first fruits of those who have*
> *died. For since death came through a human being, the resurrection of the dead*
> *has also come through a human being; for as all die in Adam, so all will be made*
> *alive in Christ. (1 Corinthians 15:19-22)*

MY PREYERS

MY PRAYERS

_____

_____

_____

_____

_____

_____

_____

Nightly News

Who needs reality TV? All you need to do is watch the nightly news, and there's more than enough reality: sad, strange, scary, and disturbing. There are the ravages of violence, disease, lack of health care, unemployment, the widening gap between rich and poor. It's enough to keep you awake nights. Maybe it should. And yet, in the midst of all of this, there are signs of hope. The Word on the street is that God's Kingdom, the one of peace, justice and love, begins here, with you.

✤ How Could It, How Can I?

How could such tragedies happen in your world, God? I don't understand how there can be so much war, hunger, oppression, natural disasters, homelessness. And how and why did we humans contribute to all this? I don't understand that either. I don't suppose I ever will. All I can do is to try in some way, in my way, however small it seems, to make things better. I don't know how to do that either, Hope of the World, so help me find that way.

> *They will hunger no more, and thirst no more; the sun will not strike them, nor any scorching heat; for the Lamb at the center of the throne will be their shepherd, and he will guide them to springs of the water of life, and God will wipe every tear from their eyes. (Revelation 7:16-17)*

✳ Greatness Unfulfilled

You'd think with all this time awake, God, with all these extra hours, I'd have achieved some kind of greatness: written the great American novel, painted a picture that changes the world's perception, composed a concerto, discovered a cure for the common cold, or done something to further world peace and justice. Well, maybe the first four are out of my reach. But that last one? That one's not the work of a single gifted hand, but the work of many hands, ordinary and otherwise, including mine. Help me find ways to join my hands to those others doing your work.

> But let justice roll down like waters,
> and righteousness like an ever-flowing stream. (Amos 5:24)

✳ Dis-Spirited and Spirit

God, sometimes it's dispiriting. Some people try so hard, and so well, to help make your world a little better. Even I try—sometimes—in my own small ways. But still, sometimes it just doesn't look as if any of this is working. But in your time, and in your way, sovereign God, you see the outcome. When I feel most dispirited, I can only pray, "Come, Holy Spirit, warm the hearts of all with the fire of your love. Send forth your Spirit and we will be reborn. And you will renew the face of the earth."

> I have said these things to you while I am still with you. But the Advocate, the Holy Spirit, whom the Father will send in my name, will teach you everything and remind you of all that I have said to you. Peace I leave with you; my peace I give to you, I do not give it to you as the world gives. Do not let your hearts be troubled, and do not let them be afraid. (John 14:25-27)

MY PRAYERS

_____

_____

_____

_____

Perspective

There is a beautiful interfaith prayer well known to many: "God grant me the serenity to accept the things I cannot change; courage to change the things I can; and wisdom to know the difference." The prayer originated with theologian Reinhold Niebuhr and later became popular through the work of Alcoholics Anonymous. For a near perfect statement on perspective, it is hard to beat. There are things you can't change, at least for the time being. But you can change the way you look at them and that in itself brings change.

❈ Openness and Integrity

Wondrous God, grant me fresh perspective so I can see things in your light. Grant me the gift of openness to the possibilities it brings. And grant me the gifts of integrity and generosity of spirit in the ways I respond and react.

> *Come, let us go up to the mountain of the Lord, to the house of the God of Jacob; that he may teach us his ways and that we may walk in his paths. (Micah 4:2)*

❈ Idols

Sometimes, God, I really let things get out of proportion. I set up my own little altars with my own little idols. And then I get out of sorts because it doesn't work the way it's supposed to. Faithful Guide, help me remember that where I set up those altars, there is my god. Help me keep things in proportion and save my altars for you.

> *What use is an idol once its maker has shaped it—a cast image, a teacher of lies? (Habakkuk 2:18)*

❄ Chicken and Egg

Am I busy obsessing about something quite petty because I cannot get to sleep? Or can I not get to sleep because I'm busily obsessing about something quite petty? I don't think I can sort it out right now. But come morning, Light of the World, let me see things in a clearer and better light.

I lift up my eyes to the hills—from where will my help come?
My help comes from the Lord, who made heaven and earth. (Psalm 121:1-2)

MY PRAYERS

Prayer and Presence

Many years ago, I attended a retreat where the director began each session with, "Let us place ourselves in the presence of God." I can still picture the chapel, softly lit, and the faint hint of incense. Above all, I can still hear the words. I think it is one of the better ways to begin to pray. Give it a try next time you're awake in the long hours leaning toward morning: "I place myself in the presence of God."

❊ Faith and Focus

God, sometimes it's really hard to pray—not because of the lack of faith, but because of the lack of *focus*. One minute I'm trying to be in your presence, and the next minute my mind has wandered afar due to distractions and abstractions. The more I try to evict them, the more they cling firmly in place. Ignoring them works a little better, Faithful Friend, but still…any suggestions? Maybe my inability to pray can be my prayer's beginning.

Be still, and know that I am God! (Psalm 46:10)

❊ Listening

I've been doing a lot of talking, God. I want to *listen* too. But sometimes life is so noisy, and I am so human, and you are so, well, Godly, that it can be hard to hear your voice. It's not that I want to go around demanding signs—lightning flashes across the sky; clouds that form a pictogram; a mysterious unstamped postcard, on high-quality stock saying, "Thinking of you" (although that would be nice). Divine Presence, teach me to listen for your voice.

Speak, Lord, for your servant is listening. (1 Samuel 3:9)

❖ Un-Prayer

O God, what can I do, where do I start? How do I find my way back to prayer? I'm trying—I think. But I feel as if I'm talking to myself, not to you. What am I doing wrong? Maybe not being able to pray, and wanting to pray, is the beginning of prayer. I don't know. I just know I can't seem to find a sense of your presence. I hope you can find a sense of mine. So, without being able to pray, I ask you, Hidden Presence, for prayer.

> *Likewise the Spirit helps us in our weakness; for we do not know how*
> *to pray as we ought, but that very Spirit intercedes with sighs too deep for words.*
> *(Romans 8:26)*

❖ Presence and Prayer

Sometimes in your presence, God of Mystery, words just drop away. And sometimes in your presence, I guess I just don't need them.

> *Do not cast me away from your presence, and do not take your holy spirit from me.*
> *Restore to me the joy of your salvation, and sustain in me a willing spirit.*
> *(Psalm 51:11-12)*

MY PRAYERS

Regrets

Now and then you hear people say they have no regrets, period—not about specific acts or inaction, but their life overall. Personally, I think anyone who has no regrets has been going through life without much passion or without paying enough attention. Then there is the question, "If you could do one thing over, what would you do?" Personally, I think it's a silly question. Make me an offer of twenty things or more, and we'll talk. What's your position on this?

❀ Should Have (Not)

I shouldn't have done it. I shouldn't have said it. I should have said something different. I should have done something different. They say hindsight is 20/20. But why is it sometimes so much easier, God, to see the light when it is dark? Come daylight, help me, God of Grace, to get things right with others.

> *For thus says the high and lofty one who inhabits eternity, whose name is Holy: I dwell in the high and holy place, and also with those who are contrite and humble in spirit, to revive the spirit of the humble, and to revive the heart of the contrite. (Isaiah 57:15)*

❀ Making Things Right (Sometimes)

Where I have regrets, God, I try to undo them. But some things can't be undone. People have moved on, out of my town, out of my life, or out of this world. Merciful God, where I have hurt people, where I have failed people—those I loved, even those I should have loved—help me to make amends. And where I can no longer do so, comfort them in your way. Make things right for them in your world. And when I arrive, I plan to say two words: "I'm sorry." And in the meantime, God, help me not build up more regrets.

> *Have mercy on me, O God, according to your steadfast love; according to your abundant mercy blot out my transgressions. Wash me thoroughly from my iniquity, and cleanse me from my sin. (Psalm 51:1-2)*

✺ "Engage Heart and Brain Before Activating Mouth"

Why did I say that? If I had known I was going to, I wouldn't have. Or, if I had known the effect it would have, I would have kept my mouth shut. It just sort of slipped out. Well, no, it walked out loudly and slammed the door. O God, I wish I could take it back. But words are hard to recover. Next time, God of Truth, help me put my heart and head in gear before I open my mouth.

Set a guard over my mouth, O Lord; keep watch over the door of my lips.
(Psalm 141:3)

MY PRAYERS

Relationships

Scripture speaks a lot about relationships: about friends and enemies, sibling support and sibling rivalry, parents and children, teacher and student; about compassion, oppression discipleship, love of neighbor and, always, love of God. You probably think a lot about relationships too. The ones you have, the ones you had, the ones you might have had, the ones you *wish* you hadn't, the ones you wish you had. Relationships—they can darken, and lighten, your days and nights.

✸ Attrition Contrition

Sometimes, God, it's so easy to get caught up in the business of living that I forget about opportunities for loving. But the reality is that I seem to lose more people in my life by attrition than by action. God of All Love, let not the opportunities for loving stretch into days, or weeks…or years. Help me to live tomorrow as a loving person. That's all I ask for: tomorrow. And then we can talk about the next day, and the day after that.

> *Beloved, let us love one another, because love is from God; everyone who loves is born of God and knows God. (1 John 4:7)*

✸ Valentine's Day

For the gift of loving and being loved, O God, I am truly thankful. Let me grow in generosity of heart and spirit to others, so that I may honor this love.

> *Sustain me with raisins, refresh me with apples; for I am faint with love.*
> *(Song of Solomon 2:5)*

Un-Valentine's Day

Everybody but me seems to have somebody, God. And here I am, alone, on Valentine's day. No romantic card. No flowers. No scented candles. No heart-shaped box of candy. Well, I do have candy...but I bought it myself. God of My Heart, help me to remember that even if I don't *have* somebody, I *am* somebody. And I am not alone. Your love is a promise I can always count on.

But by the grace of God I am what I am,
and his grace toward me has not been in vain. (1 Corinthians 15:10)

MY PRAYERS

Resentment and Anger

Anger is a two-edged sword. It can help produce some of the best and some of the worst results. Anger at injustice, tempered by compassion and wisdom, can bring about much needed social change. Unexpired anger, at almost anything, can bring disaster. Resentment can either bring nothing at all—or it can contribute to smoldering anger. Anger tends to burn hot and quick and sometimes powerfully. Resentment burns lower and longer. And for that reason it can be quite dangerous because it can go ignored until it ignites something else. So when anger knocks on your door and unpacks its baggage as resentment that won't go away, it's a good time to call on the God of Grace.

✳ Channels

O God, I was angry today, really angry. And I guess I still am. I think I have a right to be angry for once. Still, my counselor and friend, help me get control of this anger, so it doesn't get control of me. Help me channel it constructively, so I can use it to make things better in some way. Not to make things worse. When it's time to let it go, God, help me let it go. And please help me see the difference between being self-righteous and being right.

> *Put away from you all bitterness and wrath and anger and wrangling and slander, together with all malice, and be kind to one another, tenderhearted, forgiving one another, as God in Christ has forgiven you. (Ephesians 4:31-32)*

✳ Taking Sides

It's not that I'm angry or resentful, God. Well, maybe I am a little annoyed. But really, that behavior, those comments, from _____ were quite inappropriate. It's not that I'm asking you to take sides. All I'm asking is that you try to see things from my point of view, or help me alter my point of view. God of Wisdom, I'm glad that I brought it to you for understanding and so that it doesn't grow into resentment that gnaws away at my soul.

> *Be angry but do not sin; do not let the sun go down on your anger, and do not make room for the devil. (Ephesians 4:26)*

✻ Brothers and Sisters

I really like the thought of you, God, as Father, as Mother, who sent your Son to live among us. On the other hand, it really extends the meaning of family. Does this mean I have to love even those I don't know? And worse, even those I don't like? All right, all right, I get it. So, as I pray for my immediate family, I pray for my distant, or distanced, brothers and sisters this night.

> *I therefore, the prisoner in the Lord, beg you to lead a life worthy of the calling to which you have been called, with all humility and gentleness, with patience, bearing with one another in love, making every effort to maintain the unity of the Spirit in the bond of peace. (Ephesians 4:1-3)*

MY PRAYERS

Sleep and Relaxation

It's one thing to learn what to do when you can't sleep. It's another realm altogether to learn how to sleep better. There are a lot of books and articles you could read. But sleep can still remain elusive. I don't pretend to add anything new under the sun—or, in this case, the moon. But I can share with you some of my prayers about sleep.

❋ Night and Day

I close my eyes. I open them. Turn over. Stretch out. But Sleep will not come. How is it that I can be so drowsy at 3:00 p.m. and so wide awake at 3:00 a.m.? God, you are the Alpha and Omega. You created the light and the darkness. You ordered the day and the night. Couldn't we do a little bit better in ordering mine?

> *Then God said, "Let there be light"; and there was light. And God saw that the light was good; and God separated the light from the darkness. God called the light Day, and the darkness he called Night. And there was evening and there was morning, the first day. (Genesis 1:3-5)*

❋ Breath, Life, Spirit

Breathe in, breathe out. In and out, deep and slow. Take in fresh healing air. Breathe out the stress of the day. Creator God, you breathed life into Eve and Adam. Your Spirit breathes life into dry bones. Send forth your Spirit this night to breathe new life into me now and in the coming tomorrows.

> *Then he said to me, "Prophecy to the breath, prophecy, mortal, and say to the breath: Thus says the Lord God: Come from the four winds, O breath, and breathe upon these slain, that they may live." I prophesied as he commanded me, and the breath came into them, and they lived, and stood on their feet, a vast multitude. (Ezekiel 37:9-10)*

❈ Back Again

It may sound like a strange thing to say, God, but if my insomnia were suddenly cured, I think I would miss our nighttime conversations. Sometimes—too many times—I get myself so distracted with daytime things that there seems to be no time to stop and say, "Hello, remember me?" Or maybe just to sit quietly in your presence. It is a kind of lifeline. So yes, I would miss it. On the other hand, Eternal Friend, where is it written that I can't have these conversations by daylight, instead of during the watches of the night?

> *Let me hear of your steadfast love in the morning, for in you I put my trust. Teach me the way I should go, for to you I lift up my soul. (Psalm 143:8)*

MY PRAYERS

Unappreciated, Depreciated Me

You've probably had days when you feel as if people don't appreciate you as much as they "should"—or at least not as much as you would like them to. And sometimes you don't admit it for fear of feeling worse, or worse yet, sounding as if you're whining. This is one of the luxuries of bringing your feelings to prayer: God already knows what's in your heart, so you can feel safe putting it into words.

✽ Left Out

Now and then, I feel as if I'm back in seventh grade, God, and not chosen for the team or not invited to the party. I'm surprised at how hurt I can still feel at being left out. And yes, God, sometimes I've been the one leaving out another. In and Out are hard things. So, here I am, back in school again, Teacher. What do you want me to learn?

Woe is me! For I have become like one who, after the summer fruit has been gathered, after the vintage has been gleaned, finds no cluster to eat; there is no first-ripe fig for which I hunger. (Micah 7:1)

✽ Thanks, But No Thanks

It's not that I expected praise for what I did…of course not. Well, maybe just a little. But it does seem as if everyone else gets credit for what they do, God. Except me. Yes, it was worth doing in itself. But still, could I enjoy just a small, subtle taste of appreciation? Is that asking so much, Giver of All Things?

Am I now seeking human approval, or God's approval? Or am I trying to please people? If I were still pleasing people, I would not be a servant of Christ. (Galatians 1:10)

Favorites

O God, the world is so big, so complex and so competitive that sometimes I feel almost invisible, lost in the landscape of the ordinary day-to-day. That may well be where I belong—where life is lived. But to tell the truth, God, between you and me, at least now and then, I'd rather feel special. And maybe I am. I've thought about this, and sometimes I figure that somehow, with you being God—the God of Mystery and Majesty, along with being the God of Infinite Love—each one of us is your favorite. And I guess that's about as special as I can get.

Guard me as the apple of the eye; hide me in the shadow of your wings. (Psalm 17:8)

MY PRAYERS

Working

Work can be a burden, a bore or a blessing. You may choose what you do, you may accept what you do, or you may long to be doing something else. But whatever the specifics, one way or another, your work is a part of life—and of scripture: from Adam and Eve, who joined the ranks of workers involuntarily, to the laborers in the vineyard, who waited around hoping desperately to be hired, to Jesus, who forever raised the bar of service at the Passover supper in the Gospel of John. There is also Peter, former fisherman; Paul, lawyer, missionary and tentmaker; Phoebe, deacon; Lydia, seller of purple cloth. And then there is St. Joseph, patron of workers, artisan, dreamer, protector, none of whose words are recorded, but remembered forever as foster father of the Son of God. Work is a part of who you are—whether it's work in an office, workshop, restaurant, factory, farm, hospital, school, at home; whether it's for your family, yourself, an employer, as a volunteer—you name it. What does *how* you work (not *what* you do) say about you?

✤ Service and Servants

Whoever spoke of the joys of work, Lord, didn't work in my job. They certainly didn't work for my boss, with my co-workers, with my commute, in this building, for my pay. But then I think of those whose jobs are held up to ridicule: "Do you want fries with that?" Please, Lord Jesus, who acted as Servant, let there be respect for those who serve. And for all who labor by night, let them find rest and refreshment. And for me, open my eyes to possibilities that are sitting right in front of me. Help me to see things in your light.

> *Jesus, knowing that the Father had given all things into his hands, and that he had come from God and was going to God, got up from the table, took off his outer robe, and tied a towel around himself. Then he poured water into a basin and began to wash the disciples' feet and to wipe them with the towel that was tied around him. (John 13:3-5)*

❊ Job Satisfaction

Did you ever, my Friend Jesus, however briefly, miss your days working in Joseph's carpentry shop? Did those memories ever come back to you as you walked the roads during your public ministry? The satisfying recollections of seeing something shaped, smoothed, assembled and finished by the work of your hands? But you had other work to do. Lord, like your foster father Joseph, my work will never be well known. But I can still find quiet satisfaction in it. Lord, let me rest in peace tonight from my labors—preferably by going quickly to sleep! And tomorrow, bless the work of my spirit and hands.

> *He came to his hometown and began to teach the people in their synagogue, so that they were astounded, and said, "Where did this man get this wisdom and these deeds of power? Is not this the carpenter's son?" (Matthew 13:54-55)*

❊ The Work of My Hands and Hearts

Thank you, God, for letting me find joy today in my work. I know it's a blessing, and I know everyone is not so lucky—or blest. Although, O God, I wish they were. Great Provider, let all who labor in honest work be fairly rewarded with decent wages, hours and benefits. And yes, God, sometimes with joy.

> *Let the favor of the Lord our God be upon us, and prosper for us the work of our hands—O prosper the work of our hands! (Psalm 90:17)*

MY PREYERS

_____

_____

_____

_____

_____

_____

_____

Working Things Out, Or Plan B

One of my favorite bosses had a sign in her office that said, "Real life is what happens while you're making plans." Problem-solving is a great term, but it can makes things sound entirely too easy—like solving a crossword puzzle. Problem-solving can involve a fair amount of adaptability, work or working things out. So here's to real life, to working things out, to Plan B.

❈ Wrestling

I suppose maybe night isn't always a bad time to wrestle with problems, God. It's quieter with fewer distractions. Maybe that's why Jacob had his encounter with your angel by night. And things worked out for him, although not quite perfectly. God of My Refuge, if I'm going to wrestle by night with my problems, help me come to some kind of resolution, although preferably without too much dislocation in body or spirit. And please, God, not all night.

Jacob was left alone; and a man wrestled with him until daybreak. When the man saw that he did not prevail against Jacob, he struck him on the hip socket, and Jacob's hip was put out of joint as he wrestled with him. Then he said, "Let me go, for the day is breaking." But Jacob said, "I will not let you go, unless you bless me." So he said to him, "What is your name?" (Genesis 32:24-27)

❈ Plan B

O God, this surely was not my day, my week, my time. Things that were going well started to go badly, and things that were going badly started to get worse. And some things just seemed to be going nowhere at all. This is not the way I had planned it. This is not the way I had hoped it would be. Ingenious One, help me find Plan B.

Trust in the Lord with all your heart, and do not rely on your own insight. In all your ways acknowledge him, and he will make straight your paths. (Proverbs 3:5-6)

❈ Un-Plans

Some people plan everything out, God, in every detail. And while I know it's a good thing that somebody does, I'm not one of them. I just tend to just go along, get along—and sometimes just plain get it wrong. I don't really mind it that way. Just help me to remember, Guiding Shepherd, that I have a place in your plan and a way to find it.

Yet, O Lord, you are our Father; we are the clay, and you are our potter.
We are all the work of your hand. (Isaiah 64:8)

❈ Plan A

Yahweh, God-Beyond-Me, Omnipotent God, help me to remember that yours is always Plan A.

The plans of the mind belong to mortals,
but the answer of the tongue is from the Lord. (Proverbs 16:1)

MY PRAYERS

Welcome Morning

The word, and idea of, "morning" has taken hold of the human imagination since the dawn of time (no pun intended). It is in our music, poetry and proverbs. Our cave-dwelling ancestors probably awoke with relief that they hadn't been dinner for a large carnivore. But I suspect that they also saw the beauty of early morning—light breaking into darkness, bird songs, the pink and gold of dawn. Mornings can be admittedly difficult, especially Monday mornings. But mornings also can bring a sense of possibility, freshness, new beginnings. In each of the four Gospels, the first news of the Resurrection came in early morning, when the women enter the tomb to anoint Jesus' body and discover that he has risen and everything has changed. Hold onto this thought, in your heart, in your prayers, in your wakeful hours: Your mornings—tomorrow and the next day and the next—always hold new possibilities.

New Beginnings

God, there are times when I feel lost, when my life seems empty—a shadow of what it was, or what I had hoped it would be. It seems such an empty space of endings, when all I want is a new beginning. Maybe that's an oxymoron since it's not possible to have "old beginnings," but it's what I need. God of Beginnings, you sent forth your Spirit over the waters, the breath of life, to begin creation. Gracious God, send forth your Spirit now to me.

> *In the beginning when God created the heavens and the earth, the earth was a formless void and darkness covered the face of the deep, while a wind from God swept over the face of the waters. Then God said, "Let there be light"; and there was light. (Genesis 1:1-3)*

❀ Gardens

What shall I do in my garden tomorrow? Maybe tomorrow will be warm enough to start digging. It's been a long winter, God. The seeds and bulbs and roots have long lain hidden in darkness. Dormant—that is sleeping, or trying to, like me. I know in time the plants will appear, usually in a new, improved form, sometimes better than I had remembered. But so will the weeds. Can I do the same, O God, Source of All Life? Can I emerge a little better, improved, improving, when each morning comes? (And maybe get rid of some of those weeds?)

> I planted, Apollos watered, but God gave the growth. So neither the one who plants nor the one who waters is anything, but only God who gives the growth. The one who plants and the one who waters have a common purpose, and each will receive wages according to the labor of each. (1 Corinthians 3:6-8)

❀ Long Night's Journey into Day

O God, for the freshness of morning; for the promise of a new day; for the way the sky turns pink and gold in the east; for the smell of coffee; for the fresh scent of rain-watered earth; for birdsong and children's voices; for each day, My Hope and My Comforter, I give thanks. Each day is the beginning of another part of the Journey welcomed by the dawn.

> Besides this, you know what time it is, how it is now the moment for you to wake from sleep. For salvation is nearer to us now than when we became believers; the night is far gone, the day is near. Let us then lay aside the works of darkness and put on the armor of light. (Romans 13:11-12)

MY PRAYERS

_____

_____

_____

_____

_____

Acknowledgments

The word *gracias* in Spanish conveys multiple meanings, including thanks, grace and humor. I would like to thank some of the people who have brought me grace, sharing their spiritual and/or literary gifts.

To the initial editor of this book, Marcia Broucek, for her expert work and cooperative humor. And to Andrew Yankech, the final editor, for his eagle eye and insightful expertise.

To my children, Joe, Rosemary, Jeanne, and their spouses/significant others—Suzette, Skip, Scott—and granddaughter Jessica, for their encouragement. And especially to Rosemary who is always burdened with critiquing the first draft. And always, to my late husband, Henry J. Lambin, thank you.

To the long-ago retreat director, name long forgotten, who began each presentation with the words, "Let us place ourselves in the presence of God."

And last, but surely not least, to the people who have contributed so much in learning about spirituality and faith. I would like to thank all of my family and friends by name, but in doing so would surely omit someone who should be included. So I will limit myself to three professional laborers in the vineyard who have brought and who bring life and love to faith: Rev. Carl Dehne, S.J.; Sr. Fran Glowinski, O.S.F.; and Rev. Monte Johnson. Gracias.

OTHER PRAYER RESOURCES

Intercessions of Mercy
edited by Sr. Joy Clough

A practical approach to petitioning God's help on behalf of family members, friends, colleagues, community and business leaders, and the less fortunate around the world. 360-page leatherette cover, $19.95

Blessings and Prayers for Home and Family
Canadian Conference of Catholic Bishops

A book of short prayer services for all occasions, for family and small-group use. 362-page leatherette cover, $19.95

Prayers from Around the World and Across the Ages
Victor M. Parachin

Prayers from all the major religious traditions by a variety of prayer practitioners. 155-page paperback, $9.95

A Contemporary Celtic Prayer Book
and A Contemporary North American Prayer Book
William John Fitzgerald

Two innovative new prayer resources for the Liturgy of the Hours and other prayers. 150-page paperbacks, $9.95 and $12.95

On-the-Job Prayers
William David Thompson

101 prayers and reflections about work for Christians in every job and occupation. 115-page paperback, $9.95

Running into the Arms of God
Patrick Hannon, CSC

Twenty-one stories of prayer by one of the finest Catholic storytellers. 128-page hardcover, $17.95, paperback, $12.95

**Available from booksellers or call 800-397-2282
or visit www.actapublications.com.**